A Stoic's Guide to Conflict Resolution

Solving Problems with Calm

Table of Contents

Chapter 1. Introduction

Meet "A Stoic's Guide to Conflict Resolution: Solving Problems with Calm", your compass navigating you through the storms of discord and disagreement. This Special Report will not only equip you with the age-old wisdom of Stoic philosophy but also guide you on turning heated debates into constructive discourse. Imagine every conflict being a stepping stone to growth and every difficulty being a pathway to resilience! Blending practical advice and enlightening insights, this report will transform your approach to problem-solving, keeping you calm and composed even in the eye of a hurricane. Embarked on a fascinating journey of tranquility and poise; it's more than a report, it's a life-altering experience! So why wait? Open yourself to the idea of resolving conflicts stoically and see the world with new eyes!

Chapter 2. Understanding Stoicism and Its Origins

The underlying principles and ideology that constitute Stoicism gained traction roughly around 300 BC, enabling individuals, even today, to tackle personal struggles and external conflicts with serenity. Rooted in Hellenistic philosophy, Stoicism educates us on translating hardships into opportunities for growth and resilience.

2.1. The Birth of Stoicism

The origins of Stoicism can be traced back to an Athenian named Zeno of Citium. After facing a dreadful shipwreck and losing all his possessions, Zeno stumbled upon a book about Socrates in Athens, which changed the course of his life. His newfound passion for philosophy led him to form his own school, Stoicism, named after the Stoa Poikile, the painted porch in Athens where Zeno used to teach.

Stoicism was less of an academic discipline and more of a practical philosophy designed to help people live their best lives. Its goal was not just knowledge for the sake of knowledge, but knowledge applied for the betterment of self and society. Stoicism taught the art of leading a balanced life, emphasizing virtues like wisdom, courage, justice, and self-control.

2.2. Primary Tenets of Stoicism

Understanding Stoicism necessitates dissecting its fundamental tenets. Although there are numerous facets to Stoicism, three central doctrines arise:

1. The Dichotomy of Control The Stoics profoundly believed in the dichotomy of control, which separates elements of life into two

categories: things we can control and things we cannot. Stoics advocate focusing our time, energy, and efforts only on the things within our control - our actions, thoughts, judgments, and responses.

2. The Virtuous Life is the Best Life The Stoics revered the four cardinal virtues - wisdom, courage, justice, and temperance (or self-control). They perceived these virtues as interconnected elements of a virtuous life.

3. Apatheia Stoics aspired to attain a state of complete tranquility called apatheia. This state was characterized by unyielding tranquility, free of destructive emotions such as fear, envy, and frustration that could disrupt one's peace.

2.3. Stoic Philosophers

Over the years, Stoicism was carried forward and expanded upon by several philosophers. The most prominent among them were Seneca, Epictetus, and Marcus Aurelius.

Seneca, born in 4 BC, was a renowned playwright, statesman, and advisor to the Roman emperor Nero. His poignant writings on Stoicism were compiled under 'Letters from a Stoic' and 'On the Shortness of Life,' indicating how Stoicism can be integrated into daily life.

Epictetus was born into slavery around 50 AD. Despite his initial circumstances, he gained fame as a philosopher after gaining freedom. His teachings, comprising the Enchiridion and Discourses, detail the core principles of Stoic philosophy.

Marcus Aurelius, a Roman emperor from 161 to 180 AD, was widely recognized as a philosopher king. His reflections, often written during military campaigns, were later compiled into 'Meditations.' These thoughts are still considered a vital resource for understanding Stoic philosophy.

2.4. Transition and Influence

The impact of Stoicism didn't wane with the decline of the Roman Empire. Stoicism's principles found their way into various aspects of society and culture, including Christian theology, Renaissance thought, and modern psychotherapy. Cognitive-Behavioral Therapy (CBT), for instance, utilizes central stoic philosophies, focusing on the controllable aspects of negative situations – our perceptions and reactions.

In the modern world, Stoicism continues to inspire a vast array of people, such as athletes, entrepreneurs, psychologists, and individuals seeking solace and guidance in times of turmoil. Its emphasis on mindfulness, resilience, gratitude, and acceptance holds universal appeal, empowering its practitioners to lead a balanced and fulfilling life.

Understanding Stoicism, thus, requires acknowledging its origins, philosophy, and cultural transition. It offers a simplistic yet profound approach to life, enabling its followers to be unperturbed by conflict while steeping themselves in tranquility, resilience, and virtue.

Chapter 3. Key Principles of Stoic Philosophy

Stoicism, once the philosophy of the marketplace and the political arena, is a pragmatic approach towards living that has survived through centuries. Its longevity is largely due to its practical applications in everyday life, which bring peace, resilience, and strong ethical guidance.

3.1. Understanding the Foundation

The doctrine of Stoic philosophy is rooted in a practical, pragmatic approach to life and emphasizes the practice of virtue as the chief good. Foundations of Stoic thought were laid by the likes of Zeno of Citium and expanded upon by eminent philosophers like Seneca, Epictetus, and Marcus Aurelius. They proposed a way of life focusing on self-control, inner peace, and resilience in the face of adversity.

The Stoic philosophy can be traced back to its fundamental principles: the dichotomy of control, living according to nature, and the four cardinal virtues.

3.2. Dichotomy of Control

Epictetus, a significant voice in Stoic philosophy, stressed the dichotomy of control: the idea that some things are within our control, while others are not. This powerful concept informs Stoic thought significantly.

Understanding the dichotomy of control tells us where to expend our energy. Things within our control, like our judgments, decisions, desires, and aversions, should be the focus of our attention. Things beyond our control, such as the world around us, other people's actions, and the reality of our past, should not dictate our peace of mind or happiness.

The ability to discern what we can change and accept what we cannot is pivotal to attaining Stoic tranquility. It fosters resilience by letting us focus on our reactions to external events rather than the events themselves.

3.3. Living According to Nature

In the Stoic philosophy, "living according to nature" does not refer to a retreat into the wilderness but rather adherence to our essential nature as rational beings. The Stoics argued that to live a fulfilling life, we should align ourselves with nature's rationality and order.

This principle entails understanding the laws of nature and, subsequently, harmonizing oneself with them. Our actions must be dictated by reason and not by momentary passions, emotions, or societal pressure.

In practice, this principle prompts us to ask ourselves if we are following the pull of irrational desires or if we are acting in accordance with our reason-based human nature.

3.4. Four Cardinal Virtues

Stoic thought acknowledges the following virtues as fundamentally significant—Wisdom, Courage, Justice, and Temperance.

- Wisdom: Wisdom, in a Stoic sense, means understanding what is truly good, bad, or indifferent, all according to nature. It also means applying this understanding to our judgments and decision-making process.

- Courage: Stoic courage refers to standing by the rational decisions one has made, even in times of adversity. It's not only physical bravery but also bravery on a moral and psychological front.

- Justice: Justice, for the Stoics, encompasses our relationships with others—being fair, treating others with dignity, and acting for the common good.

- Temperance: Temperance is a principle of restraint or moderation. It involves managing our desires and impulses by not succumbing to extremes and by prioritizing rationality.

Understanding, acknowledging, and striving for these virtues leads us to eudaimonia, a Greek term usually translated as flourishing or the good life. It allows us to maintain tranquility and composure, even amidst conflict or chaos.

3.5. Practical Applications of Stoic Philosophy

Stoic philosophy was meant to be applied, not just discussed. From meditations to negative visualization, Stoicism offers practical tools to navigate life's storms.

- Meditations: These consist of reflecting on the principles of Stoicism and considering how they can be applied to our lives. Marcus Aurelius's 'Meditations' is an excellent example of this practice, illustrating how these principles guided his actions.

- Premeditatio malorum (negative visualization): This is contemplating potential difficulties or adversities to prepare oneself for adverse circumstances.

- Voluntary discomfort: This practice involves deliberately experiencing minor discomforts to build mental stamina and resilience, thus preparing oneself for unexpected adversities.

Stoicism isn't about suppressing emotions, but about transforming our relationship with them to live a flourishing life. By integrating these fundamental principles of Stoic philosophy in your mindset, you can navigate through the chaos and discord of life with calmness and reason, turning each conflict into constructive growth.

Chapter 4. Stoicism and Conflict: How Do They Connect?

Before delving into the connection between Stoicism and conflict, it's essential to understand what Stoicism is. Stoicism, originating in Athens in the 3rd century BC, is a philosophical approach to life that emphasizes virtue (the highest good) and teaches that happiness is found in accepting the moment as it is, not allowing ourselves to be controlled by our desires for pleasure or our fear of pain. Stoics believed that by developing an understanding of the natural world and our place within it, we could lead fulfilled and tranquil lives.

4.1. The Stoic Frame of Mind

The basis of Stoicism is the ability to separate what is within our control and what is not. Stoic philosophers believed that we cannot control or rely on anything external for our happiness or misery. The only thing truly under our control is our thoughts and reactions. This ability to differentiate and focus solely on what we can control is what prepares the Stoic mind for conflict.

Indeed, conflict typically arises when people vie for control, whether of resources, power, or authority. To a Stoic, these are external factors that are intrinsically uncontrollable and thus not worthy of anxiety or worry. A Stoic understands that the only power they truly hold is how they react to the conflict. Will they let it disturb their peace, leading to more conflict? Or will they choose to respond calmly, effectively minimizing the negative impact?

4.2. The Stoic Approach to Conflict

When it comes to conflict resolution, the Stoic approach emphasizes calm,composed reasoning, and constructive engagement. A Stoic would first seek to understand the root cause of the conflict. Once that's established, they would attempt to remedy the problem, not exacerbate it.

According to the Stoics, viewing conflicts as challenges to overcome rather than threats to our serenity is key. This frame of mind shifts our attention from being defensive to seeking a solution, fostering dialogue instead of argument.

Furthermore, understanding the impermanent nature of external circumstances and irrational responses allows a Stoic to tolerate disagreement and discord. They understand that conflicts are inevitable but also temporary parts of life, and as such, they choose to act rather than react.

4.3. Embracing Discomfort and Developing Resilience

One of the fundamental tenets of Stoicism is training oneself to be comfortable with discomfort. This might seem counterintuitive, but when applied to conflicts, it can inculcate resilience. It is by facing and dealing with conflicts, rather than avoiding them, that we grow stronger and more adept at handling future adversarial circumstances.

Stoicism advises that we consider every difficult encounter - be it a heated discussion or a full-blown disagreement - as an opportunity to practice patience, restraint, and empathy. Instead of viewing the conflict as a personal attack or an unfair situation, the Stoic would view it as a chance to learn and grow.

4.4. Empathy and Understanding in Stoicism

Empathy is central to the Stoic philosophy, particularly when dealing with conflicts. Stoics believe that most conflicts arise from misunderstanding or distorted perceptions. Therefore, understanding others' perspectives and emotions can diffuse hostility and open avenues for dialogue.

Stoics look at the bigger picture, understanding that everyone has their reasons for acting or thinking a certain way. Instead of becoming defensive or feeling attacked, they try to understand the other person's point of view. This, in turn, opens the path to compassion and mutual respect, key ingredients for positive, peaceful conflict resolution.

Stoicism indeed provides an evolved framework for addressing conflicts without sacrificing tranquility or integrity. Its principles can guide us through the tumultuous waters of discord, helping us maintain composure and balance while navigating towards resolution. Accepting the inevitability of conflict, viewing it as an opportunity for growth, and demonstrating compassion and understanding towards our opposers are monumental steps towards solving problems in a calm and collected manner. Ultimately, Stoicism teaches us not just how to weather the storm, but to appreciate it for the strength it brings.

In conclusion, Stoicism and conflict are intrinsically interconnected, reminding us that conflicts are natural occurrences and that our response to them is entirely within our control. The way we react to and resolve these disagreements is crucial in our pursuit of virtue, peace, and self-improvement. With the wisdom of Stoicism, we not only navigate conflicts but turn them into pathways to resilience and personal growth.

Chapter 5. Adopting a Stoic Mindset: The First Step towards Calm Resolution

It all starts with an idea. A notion that propels us towards a way of thinking that is contrary to what we might have been conditioned to believe. The Stoics understood that life was composed of many challenges, but instead of reacting emotionally, they chose to respond with reason and thoughtfulness. They believed in the power of a rational mind and its ability to navigate through the turbulent sea of life's conflicts and challenges.

So, let us embark on eluding fear, and stress by embracing a stoic mindset. This transformative journey comprises many components, and we will explore the five primary aspects of embodying a stoic mindset: Perception, Judgement, Actions, Will, and Mindfulness.

5.1. Perception: Crafting a New Lens

Stoic philosophy starts with shaping our perception. It is the foundation upon which we build our thoughts and actions. It is not the event that disturbs people, but their judgment concerning the event. To change the lens through which we perceive our surroundings and situations, characterizes the primary step towards bringing about the drastic transformation promised by stoicism.

Perception, from a stoic point of view, involves understanding that the world outside is independent of our mind. We may not have control over the things that happen, but we certainly have a say in how we perceive them. And by altering our perception, not only can we handle situations better, but we can also shift our reactions, transforming them from destructive to constructive.

To see the world from a Stoic's perspective, it's not about ignoring the negatives or glossing over the problems we encounter. It's about recognizing these issues, understanding the emotions they arouse, and then choosing a different path - a path that leads us to equilibrium, not conflict.

5.2. Judgement: Guiding our Internal Compass

Once we've begun to understand our perception, it's essential to turn our focus inward. That's where we find judgment, the compass that guides us. Without proper judgment, even an optimally crafted perception might falter.

In our everyday life, we encounter countless moments where our judgments guide our reactions. We need to pause, re-evaluate our biases and allow room for dissent in our thoughts. Are our judgments leading us towards harmony or kindling unnecessary conflicts? Remember, finding the answer cogently will pivot us towards embodying a truly stoic mindset.

Remember, each encounter, each event you face, serves as a personal test for your ability to stay grounded, demonstrating wisdom and tranquility. Practicing stoic judgment involves reminding yourself of the impermanence of everything, presenting you with an opportunity to grow rather than simply react.

5.3. Actions: The Manifestation of Mindset

Actions speak louder than words. This phrase rings true especially when adopting a Stoic mindset. Our actions reflect our internal dialogue, displaying clearly the purity of our stoic perceptions and judgments.

Emulating a Stoic warrior in times of conflict involves practicing the virtues of courage, wisdom, temperance and justice, making tough choices and standing by them, even when the tides are against us. Step back during moments of discord and ask yourself - "Is this action aligned with my stoic principles?" Remember, your actions should always be in accordance with nature and reason.

As you immerse deeper into your stoic mindset, your actions will germinate from a place of tranquil understanding rather than reactive thoughts. Stoicism brings forward the aspect of acting with a sense of duty, without anticipating any rewards. When you adopt a Stoic's set of virtues, you naturally navigate yourself towards a calm and insightful resolution of conflicts.

5.4. Will: The Inner Resilience

Stoic philosophy primarily revolves around the concept of control - distinguishing between what we can and cannot control. The will is one such thing that's fully within our control. The core principle of stoicism involves aligning our will with nature. Here, nature can be interpreted as the natural order of the universe and our role within it. Remember, fortune can take away all our external possessions, but it cannot touch our will, our character.

It is our will that transforms our perception and judgment into action. It provides us with the inner resilience, the robustness to cope with life's challenges. By aligning our will with the natural order, by accepting the world as it is, we empower ourselves to navigate life with equanimity.

5.5. Mindfulness: The Magic of the Present Moment

Mindfulness is the practice of being aware and present in the moment without judgment. For Stoics, it serves as the lifeline that ties all perceptions, judgments, actions, and our will together. Being present allows us to examine our thoughts, words, and deeds with a clear mind.

Mindfulness techniques can help us carry out daily life activities with our full presence, giving us the power to engage with our thoughts, feelings, judgments, and actions coherently. We will be able to observe our mind's tendencies, understand its patterns, and mindfully alter them towards a stoically calm resolution.

Stoic mindfulness also propagates the impermanence of everything – understanding that every circumstance is ephemeral, and change is the only constant allows us to maintain our poise in the face of adversity.

As we conclude this chapter, remember to imbibe these principles into your daily routines. Molding a new lens of perception, refining our judgments, ensuring our actions mirror our mindset, fortifying our will, and practicing the art of mindfulness will serve as the stepping stones to achieving conflict resolution the stoic way. Transforming the principles highlighted in these pages into a practical reality requires patience and constant practice. We might falter at times, but don't be perturbed. After all, adopting a stoic mindset is a lifelong journey, and every journey starts with the first step!

Chapter 6. Equipping Your Stoic Toolkit: Techniques for Conflict Resolution

In the realm of Stoic philosophy, preparing your mind is the first step towards approaching any circumstances, especially conflicts, with a calm and composed demeanor. Thus, let us begin our quest by equipping your Stoic toolkit with potent philosophical principles and practical techniques.

6.1. The Core Stoic Principles

Philosophy often provides the principles we need to face life's trials. Stoicism, as one such philosophy, offers a wealth of wisdom in conflict resolution. Here are four core Stoic principles that will serve as the foundation of your toolkit:

1. **The Dichotomy of Control:** Recognize what is within your control and what is not. Your actions, judgments, and responses are within your control, whereas the actions and reactions of others are not.

2. **Virtuous Actions are the Only Goods:** In stoic philosophy, virtue is the sole good. Among virtues are wisdom, courage, justice (fairness), and self-control.

3. **Emotions Result from Judgments:** We are not distressed by events themselves but by our perception of them. It's not what happens to us, but our reaction to it that matters.

4. **Acceptance:** Accept life as it comes, and adapt accordingly. Accepting doesn't mean resigning or giving up, but rather understanding the nature of life and adjusting our actions accordingly.

6.2. The Tranquil Mind: Mastery Over Emotions

One crucial aspect of the Stoic philosophy is mastering your emotions. A clear, tranquil mind is likely to resolve conflicts more successfully because it can view the situation objectively and without the biases and distortions that strong emotions can cause. Here is a four-step technique you can use:

1. **Identify:** Recognize when you're having a powerful emotional reaction to a situation.

2. **Reflect:** Consider why you're reacting in such a way. Is it truly reflective of the situation, or is it an overreaction based on past experiences or unconscious biases?

3. **Deconstruct:** Once you understand why you're reacting, you can deconstruct your emotional response. This involves questioning the validity of your emotions and judgments, allowing you to disengage your feelings from the situation.

4. **Reframe:** The final step is to reframe the situation in a more rational and objective light.

6.3. The Four Virtues: Implementing Virtuous Actions

The Stoic philosophy identifies wisdom, courage, justice, and temperance as four primary virtues. Here is how you can exercise these virtues in conflict resolution:

1. **Wisdom:** This virtue encompasses good judgment, discretion, and the faculty to discern the feasible from the infeasible. In conflict resolution, it's wise to take a step back from the situation, consider all perspectives, and make a well-informed decision.

2. **Courage:** In delicate conflict situations, one needs to have moral courage to stand by what is right, even if it isn't the popular opinion.

3. **Justice:** It involves fairness, treating each party involved without prejudice. You need to ensure you're creating a space where everyone feels heard and respected.

4. **Temperance:** Essentially, this virtue signifies balance and self-control. In conflicts, one should practice to exercise restraint and not let emotions overpower rational, balanced decision-making.

6.4. The Reflective Stoic: A Practical Exercise

Journaling is often recommended in Stoic practices for self-reflection and awareness. It's an effective tool to observe one's feelings without judgment and to enhance one's self-awareness. Here's a method of journaling for conflict resolution:

1. **Situation:** Write down the conflict situation in as much detail as possible.

2. **Feelings:** Write down your feelings about the situation. Be as honest as possible with yourself at this stage.

3. **Evaluate:** Review the conflict in light of the dichotomy of control. What was under your control in this situation? What wasn't? What can you do differently?

4. **Refine:** Examine the situation under the lens of the four virtues. How can you implement wisdom, courage, justice, and temperance in future conflicts?

6.5. The Stoic Meditator: Visualization Techniques

In the Stoic practice, visualization is a popular tool. Not to be confused with positive visualization, the Stoic form of visualization is mental preparation for potential disappointment or conflict. This practice, known as premeditatio malorum or negative visualization, can prove particularly helpful in conflict resolution. Here's a guide to practice it:

1. **Imagine:** Think of a situation that might lead to conflict. Visualize it happening in your mind's eye.

2. **Feel:** Allow yourself to experience the emotions that might arise in such a situation.

3. **Respond:** Now, armed with your Stoic tools, imagine how you should respond.

4. **Reflect:** Notice the difference between how you would have reacted before and how you would now respond as a Stoic.

Our exploration above unveils the core principles and practical techniques of Stoic philosophy that you can apply for effective conflict resolution. By internalizing these profound lessons and practicing Stoic exercises daily, you are walking on a path that not only navigates you through conflicts but also bestows upon you equanimity and resilience. This toolkit is your dependable companion, guiding you toward tranquility and strength, turning every conflict into an opportunity for growth and understanding.

Chapter 7. The Art of Listening: Stoicism's Silent Strategy

Listening, a fundamental aspect of human communication, often doesn't receive the attention it deserves. We take our ability to hear for granted and mistake it for the skill of active listening. We forget that hearing is an involuntary physiological function, whereas listening is a voluntary mental function that requires our explicit effort. To the Stoics, listening is an art form - a silent strategy to gain insights and wisdom.

7.1. The Underrated Skill

True listening requires discarding your biases and judgments, opening your mind, and fully immersing yourself in what the other person is saying, free from interference of your own thoughts and feelings.

"Most people do not listen with the intent to understand; they listen with the intent to reply." Stephen R. Covey's statement mirrors the widespread behavioral malfunction we perceive as listening. Lying at the root of many conflicts, this skewed form of engagement must be corrected.

Stoicism pushes for a more thoughtful, attentive mode of interaction. By deliberately quieting our minds and focusing on the speaker, we shift from passive receivers of information to active participants in a three-dimensional dialogue involving verbal cues, body language, and emotional undercurrents.

7.2. Understanding, Not Responding

Marcus Aurelius, the famous Stoic emperor, once said, "We have two ears and one mouth so that we can listen twice as much as we speak." The core of this wisdom is in the recognition that understanding far surpasses speaking in importance.

Instead of formulating responses while someone else is speaking, true listening entails total absorption of the speaker's words, their context, and the sentiments behind them. A stoic listener suspends their own judgment, opinions, and thoughts, allowing the speaker's perspective to exist as it is, without rushing in to interpret or correct.

7.3. Embracing Silence

Embracing silence is an integral part of effective listening. In this increasingly noisy world, silence is often feared and misinterpreted as awkwardness. However, in Stoicism, silence is revered - an arena hosting undisturbed thought. Listeners should perceive silence not as a chance to speak but as a breather for understanding, assessment, and synthesis of information.

Silence does not equate to absence. It's a potent tool that can do wonders for the listener's comprehension and the speaker's willingness to share more. The power it holds in bridging gaps between individuals in a conflict can be extraordinary when rightly utilized.

7.4. The Power of Empathy

When we genuinely listen, we interact with empathy. Stoicism focuses strongly on our common humanity and our duty to treat each other with kindness and respect. This involves empathic listening, which means offering a non judgmental ear and acknowledging the speaker's feelings.

By doing so, we create a secure atmosphere for open communication. This positive space is critical in conflict resolution as it promotes mutual respect, understanding, and assurance, which are key to peaceful resolutions.

7.5. Listening as a Mode of Learning

Following the principles of Stoicism, deep listening goes beyond lending an ear to the obvious; it's a receptacle for knowledge. "Applied wisdom," after all, is the ultimate goal of Stoic philosophy, and this cannot be achieved without gaining new insights — and one of the most efficient ways to do so is by truly listening.

A stoic listener is an eternal student, adopting a mindset of curiosity and learning. This approach invites a treasure of wisdom and fosters a habit of continuous intellectual and emotional growth.

7.6. Bringing it All Together

Incorporate these tenets of Stoic art of listening into your everyday life. Be present in your conversations. Listen, not merely to respond, but to understand. Brace the silence, do not fear it. Employ empathy in your communication. Continuously learn from every dialogue you partake in.

Above all, remember, the journey toward mastering an art is always gradual. Practice with patience and steadfastness, for it is the culmination of these small but steady steps that lead towards a big change. Transform yourself into a respectful, empathic participant in all your interactions and watch your conflicts diffuse into a more cooperative and meaningful discourse.

Embodying these Stoic approaches will not only strengthen your listening skills but will also lead you towards an enlightened path of conflict resolution — one where with every word heard, every meaning understood, every silences embraced, and every emotion empathized, you grow a little more, becoming a kinder, understanding, and wiser version of yourself.

Chapter 8. Assertiveness and Respect: Balancing Your Reactions

We commence by unraveling an often misunderstood concept: assertiveness. Numerous times, assertiveness is mistaken for aggressiveness; however, there is a significant distinction. Assertiveness stems from a place of respect—for oneself and for others—while aggressiveness is a reactionary emotional burst, often lacking in consideration for others. Hence, to comprehend how a stoic might approach the balancing act of assertiveness and respect, it's necessary we first comprehend this.

8.1. Understanding Assertiveness

It's vital, within conflict resolution, to realize that assertiveness is not about insisting on your point of view or bulldozing over others' viewpoints. Rather, it's about articulating thoughts, feelings, and needs in an open, direct, and respectful manner. Stoics believed that the way we perceive and respond to events is within our control. In the context of assertiveness, this implies managing our responses not reactively but proactively, and expressing disagreement or needs without resorting to anger or passive-aggressiveness.

8.2. Employing Stoic Philosophy in Assertiveness

Stoics espouse that the cornerstone of sane thinking is to shape your world internally and not let the external world disturb the tranquility within. This necessitates staying assertive about our mental boundaries. To be assertive, a stoic might utilize the practice of rational decision making, keeping emotions in check, and ensuring their personal boundaries aren't violated unfairly.

8.3. Assertiveness: A Marker of respect

Being assertive calls for unwavering respect but also evokes it. The act of asserting your viewpoint while valuing others' opinions sends a clear message: you value diversity in thought and approach. This in turn cultivates an atmosphere of mutual respect, a foundation on which constructive conversations can occur and conflicts genuinely resolve.

8.4. Role of Empathy in Assertiveness

Being empathetic doesn't mean conceding your position or relinquishing your assertiveness; instead, it facilitates the direction of the conversation into more productive paths. It allows us, as the Stoics championed, to control our response while understanding the others' viewpoint, creating space for a balanced dialogue that integrates both assertiveness and respect.

8.5. Balancing Assertiveness and Being Respectful

Here, we might take cues from the precepts of Stoicism. In balancing assertiveness and respect, a Stoic perspective would involve understanding our control sphere, thinking logically about the situation, and maintaining tranquility regardless of external circumstances. It's navigating through conflict by respecting your emotions and those of others, not letting transitory feelings cloud judgment, and keeping actions in alignment with virtues of wisdom, courage, justice, and temperance.

8.6. Nurturing Assertiveness: Developing Self-Awareness

A pivotal step in nurturing assertiveness involves knowing oneself deeply. Stoics suggest continuous self-questioning as a means of self-growth—to identify the roots of your reactions, your triggers and biases. Understanding these is to understand the variables that hinder balanced assertiveness.

8.7. Assert your Boundaries, But Respect Others'

Meaningful conflict resolution does not involve the dissolution of one's self or principles. As Stoics, we assert our boundaries while refraining from crossing others'. Walk the line between maintaining your stance and respecting conflicting views. Disagreements cease to be personal battles and become opportunities for shared understanding and growth.

This perspective may seem challenging to embody, especially amidst conflict. Yet, adopting this Stoic approach of balancing assertiveness with mutual respect in conflict resolution can cultivate a more serene, fair, and constructive environment in stark contrast to the turmoil engagements often result in.

8.8. Act, Don't React

The Stoic philosophy does not advocate passivity. Being stoic means recognizing situations as they are and taking righteous action, not being devoid of emotion but mastering them to act rather than react.

In essence, it's about using your rationality to channel assertiveness and evoke respect naturally.

8.9. Conclusion

While no one technique ensures successful conflict resolution, incorporating a Stoic approach, with an emphasis on balanced assertiveness and respect, can create an atmosphere conducive to constructive resolution. The Stoic philosophy serves as a guide, helping us navigate our lives calmly amid discord, and allowing us to reveal and reinforce the best version of ourselves.

Remember the Stoic wisdom: events in themselves are neutral; it's our perception and response that add color to them. Aspire to color your world with understanding, respect, and assertiveness, and witness transformations, not just in conflict resolution but in living your life itself.

Chapter 9. Playing with Perspective: Seeing Differently, Solving Differently

In any conflict or disagreement, the first impulse is often to dig our heels in, stick to our viewpoint, and convince the other person that we are right. Yet, this one-way approach seldom helps to achieve calm or effective resolution. The inability to see beyond our standpoint can lead to impasses or undue stress. Herein lies the power of perspective, the unfettered ability to expand one's vision and see situations, difficulties, or disputes through a different lens.

9.1. The Quintessential Stoic Approach

The Stoics, ancient philosophers known for their serenity in the face of adversity, had an unusual knack for perspective-taking. They believed that our response to any problem is governed by the interpretation we give to it. The more rigid our perceptions, the more confined our options become. In contrast, a flexible, panoramic view opens up opportunities for understanding, negotiation, and ultimately, resolution.

For instance, imagine you're frustrated with your colleague's constant lateness. It hinders your work and seems disrespectful. Yet, if you're only seeing this as your colleague's disregard for your time, then the only solutions appear would be confrontations or complaints. Instead, a wider, Stoic perspective might include considerations like: Is there something happening in their personal life? Are they juggling multiple responsibilities at work? Are they aware of the impact of their lateness? Incorporating a panoramic view like this can lead to a more empathetic conversation or a structure that accommodates their circumstances.

9.2. Shifting Perspectives: Theory Vs. Practice

The idea of changing one's viewpoint sounds reasonable, but applying it amidst conflict can be challenging. Any threat to our values, opinions, and norms can cause anxiety, making us cling harder to our perspective. The Stoics addressed this concern through practices that shifted and widened their worldview.

One such practice was the 'View from Above.' Imagine yourself rising above the immediate conflict to see the broader scenario. Your matter of dissent may appear significant in your immediate sphere, but how big does it look from a thousand feet above? The Stoics used this method to breed humility, patience, and acceptance, all crucial elements for conflict resolution.

Consider another scenario wherein you're angry because a friend forgot your important event. Up-close, it feels like they've let you down. But imagine viewing the world from a distance, seeing all humans, each with their own complexities, all juggling numerous tasks and responsibilities. Does it somehow lessen the intensity of your anger? Does it pivot the discussion from attack-defend to a candid conversation about forgetfulness and responsibility?

9.3. Psychologists on Perspective

The Stoics weren't alone in their perspective-centric approach. Modern psychology too stresses the role of Perspective-Taking, the conscious attempt to understand and appreciate others' viewpoints.

According to research, Perspective-Taking reduces bias, promotes empathy, and enhances cooperation – all conduits of effective problem-solving. It encourages us to explore the conflict from the other person's viewpoint first and then orchestrate a solution. By doing this, it breaks the win-lose paradigm of disagreements, steering them towards a win-win resolution.

When conflicts arise, before rushing to defend your position, ask yourself, 'What might be their perspective?' 'What factors might be influencing them?' 'How might they be seeing this situation?' Such queries don't weaken your stance but foster an environment conducive to dialogue and resolution.

9.4. Perspective in Practise: Techniques for Change

While understanding the theory and rationale behind perspective shift is easy, implementing it can be challenging. Here are some techniques that can assist in this journey.

1. Reframe: Make it a habit to reframe problems in various ways. A 'late' colleague could be an opportunity for planning your work better. A 'forgetful' friend could be a chance for a heartfelt discussion on prioritizing.

2. Listen Actively: When involved in conflict, listen more than you talk. Engage in the conversation with the intent to understand, not just to reply.

3. Empathize: Try to empathetically consider the other person's feelings and experiences. This understanding can help you respond more effectively.

4. Practice Mindfulness: Being present and aware can help you identify your viewpoint and assess if you need to shift it.

5. Journal: Write about your conflicts or challenges from a third person's perspective. It can lead to novel insights and resolutions.

6. Seek Feedback: Often, we are blinded by our biases. Feedback from a trusted friend or a mentor can provide a different perspective on our problems.

Remember, the journey to mastering perspective-taking isn't about invalidating your viewpoint. Instead, it's about enlarging your view to accommodate multiple angles, opinions and solutions. In words of Stoic philosopher Marcus Aurelius, "Everything we hear is an opinion, not a fact. Everything we see is a perspective, not the truth." Challenge yourself to see conflicts through this multidimensional lens. That is the path to tranquil resolution.

The wisdom of the Stoics and modern psychology converges on the transformative power of 'perspective'. Equipped with this understanding and the tools to implement it, you are ready to turn conflicts into constructive growth opportunities, seeing differently, solving differently.

Chapter 10. Turning Challenges into Opportunities: The Stoic Resilience

Resilience is a fundamental aspect of Stoicism, a product of viewing any obstacle or challenge as an opportunity for growth and self-improvement. It's about responding instead of reacting, maintaining calmness and poise, and making effective decisions instead of impulsive ones. It's about engaging with life's inevitable challenges in a manner that transforms adversity into advantage.

10.1. The Stoic's Perspective on Challenges

The Stoic sees challenges not as an impediment but as a part of life — something to be addressed appropriately, rather than feared or avoided. Stoicism equips you with the strength to face challenges head-on with grace and dignity, fostering resilience in the process.

Consider the thoughts of Marcus Aurelius, one of the most famous Stoic thinkers, who once wrote, "The impediment to action advances action. What stands in the way becomes the way." This statement encapsulates the essence of Stoic resilience. With a Stoic mindset, you can transform challenges into achievements.

10.2. Gaining Strength from Stoic Wisdom

Resilience is more than an inherent trait; it's a skill that can be nurtured, refined, and strengthened continuously. The writings of ancient Stoics offer ample wisdom to foster this resilience, enhancing your capacity to deal with life's challenges.

Epictetus, a hugely influential Stoic philosopher, argued for the importance of focusing only on what is within our control. His insightful teachings remind us that, while we cannot always control the challenges that come our way, we can control our response to those challenges.

10.3. Nurturing Resilience: The Stoic Way

An essential tenet of Stoicism is understanding and accepting that life will inevitably pose challenges. But how does one nurture the resilience needed to face these hurdles with composure? Here are a few practices derived from Stoic philosophy to help build resilience:

1. Practice acceptance: Embrace life's adversities as part of the human experience. Accept that there will always be things outside of your control.

2. Rethink challenges: See challenges as opportunities for growth, not as hindrances. This shift in perspective can encourage resilience.

3. Cultivate emotional intelligence: Work on understanding and managing your emotions, which aids in thinking clearly and responding appropriately in difficult situations.

4. Strengthen self-discipline: Practice self-control and learn to resist impulsive reactions, which can amplify the perception of a challenge.

10.4. Turning Challenge into Opportunity

Embarking on the path of resilience requires turning adversity into advantage, transforming challenge into opportunity. This mindset is what distinguishes the Stoic. No matter how formidable the odds or daunting the obstruction, a Stoic remains unfazed, for they see not an obstacle, but an avenue to gain wisdom.

Here's how you can turn challenges into opportunities:

- Rethink obstacles: Learn to identify and understand the challenge you face. Recognizing the nature of the obstacle can often be the first step in overcoming it.

- Develop a plan: Once you understand the problem, devise a course of action. Consider viable solutions and determine which approach aligns best with your values and goals.

- Embrace failure: Treat failure as a lesson rather than a dead-end. Every failure provides critical insights for improvement and guides you to success.

- Stay persistent: Resilience requires patience. Remember that Rome wasn't built in a day, and neither is resilience. Persistently embrace the journey of growth.

10.5. Conclusion: The Path to Stoic Resilience

The path to Stoic resilience is a journey, not a destination. It's about steady progress and personal growth. It requires acceptance and acknowledgment of life's challenges as golden opportunities for improvement, refusing to let obstacles undermine your well-being.

Through this transformative journey, you'll not only fortify your resilience but also foster a tranquil, discerning mind that can remain unfazed by life's storms. By viewing every challenge as an opportunity, you leverage difficulties as pathways to success and serenity, demonstrating true Stoic resilience. The Stoic's guide to conflict resolution doesn't, therefore, merely offer a way to face external conflicts but also a means to resolving internal turmoil and achieving personal growth, ushering in a newfound calm in the face of life's greatest storms.

Chapter 11. Maintaining the Stoic Balance: A Pathway for Future Conflicts

Every journey begins with a single step. Here, we initialize our expedition into the profound realms of Stoic conflict resolution technique, by comprehending the art of maintaining the Stoic balance.

The concept of balance is deeply embedded in Stoic philosophy, it encapsulates the practice of disciplining our responses to external events. As Epictetus, the Stoic philosopher, rightly said, "People are not disturbed by things, but by the view they take of them." By preserving equanimity in the face of conflict, we not only strengthen our mental fortitude but also pave the path for future conflicts.

11.1. Making of a Stoic Mind: Cultivating Emotional Equilibrium

The Stoic mind is primarily an embodiment of emotional equilibrium. The Roman Stoic Seneca famously emphasized that "All cruelty springs from weakness." Therefore, the first step towards maintaining our Stoic balance is to master our emotions. Here are a few techniques:

1. Embrace the Dichotomy of Control: Recognize what lies in your control. This simple dichotomy forms the heart of Stoic thought. Acts of another, unpredictable outcomes, or the flux of circumstances, can be acknowledged, but at the same time, freeing oneself of undue influence.

2. Meditation and Visualization: Using effective meditative practices, envisage potential conflicts and visualize your

response, grounded in calmness and reason.

3. Preserve Your Inner Equanimity: Preserve your integrity as an untarnished fortress, immune to external circumstances. This practice allows us to isolate our emotional responses from the situation itself, fostering a composed mindset.

11.2. The Quintessential Stoic Approach: Reactive vs Proactive

A core trait distinguishing Stoic philosophy is the shift from reactive to proactive. Reactivity is an impulsive response to conflict. The Stoics advise a proactive approach that values careful contemplation before reacting.

1. Harnessing Impulses: We have the power to alter our reactions to conflicts. By nurturing a proactive mindset, we retain control over our responses rather than being usurped by mere reflexes.

2. Anticipating Outcomes: Develop an anticipatory attitude towards conflicts, foreseeing them as inevitable, and craft your responses accordingly. Embrace them as opportunities for growth.

3. Cultivating Perspective: Adopt a broad view towards the world, keeping in mind the transient nature of conflicts. This enables us to derive valuable lessons from every situation, thus strengthening our resilience.

11.3. Stoic Strategies for Conflict Resolution

Stoicism puts forward several strategies to combat and resolve conflicts. These strategies are not merely defensive shields but proactive swords that enable us to face any challenge and emerge stronger and wiser.

1. Pause and Reflect: Take a moment to pause and dissect the conflict. Try to unveil the deep-rooted issues and, consequently, the best way to address them.

2. Empathy over Antipathy: Practice empathy towards the other party involved in the conflict. Viewing the situation from their perspective not only helps understand their stance better but also fosters mutual respect, leading to peaceful resolution.

3. Seek the Truth: In the skirmish of conflicts, the truth often gets cloaked. The Stoic seeks to unveil the truth, discarding personal biases and prejudices.

11.4. Embracing the Stoic Balance: A Lifelong Journey

Incorporating Stoic balance into your life is no overnight transformation; rather, it's a lifelong journey of the pursuit of virtue and tranquility. So, embark on this journey equipped not just with these strategies but also with the companion of patience.

1. Patience and Persistence: The path of Stoic balance requires patience and continuous efforts. Do not become disheartened over temporary setbacks.

2. Lifelong Learning: The Stoic journey is one of lifelong learning. Every conflict, every setback is an opportunity to grow.

3. Cultivating the Virtues: Keep in mind the four cardinal virtues of Stoic philosophy - wisdom, courage, justice, and temperance. They will guide you to maintain the Stoic balance during conflicts.

In conclusion, the Stoic balance isn't just about maintaining tranquility in the face of immediate conflict; it extends much deeper and wider. It's about perpetually grounding oneself in wisdom, keeping a balanced view of life, and continually evolving one's character. That's the Stoic's pathway for future conflicts.